a

THE "SHOWN TO THE CHILDREN" SERIES

EDITED BY LOUEY CHISHOLM

BUTTERFLIES AND MOTHS

PLATE I

2

1

1. Silver-washed Fritillary
2. Pearl-bordered Fritillary

Butterflies and Moths

SHOWN TO THE CHILDREN

BY

JANET HARVEY KELMAN

DESCRIBED BY

REV. THEODORE WOOD

FORTY-EIGHT COLOURED PICTURES

LONDON & EDINBURGH

T. C. & E. C. JACK

A large number of the butterflies and moths in this book were drawn from insects in Mr. R. J. M. M'Kerrell's private collection, and the artist wishes to thank him most cordially for his great kindness.

PREFACE

IN this little book I want to tell you something about the common butterflies and moths which you may find in almost all parts of the country. But, first of all, I think that perhaps I had better say something about what we generally call their "life-history."

Of course you know that butterflies and moths are not butterflies and moths to begin with. They enter the world in the form of eggs, just as birds and fishes do. These eggs are often very beautiful indeed. You may find them on the leaves of different plants, sometimes on the upper side and sometimes on the lower side. And if you look at them through a good strong magnifying-glass—or, better still, through a microscope—you will find that some are shaped like little sugar-loaves, and some like acorns, and some like tiny melons, while they are nearly always covered with raised patterns which one might almost think must have been cut by fairy chisels.

In course of time these eggs hatch, and out come a number of little caterpillars, which at once begin to eat the leaves of the plant on which the eggs were laid. They have most wonderful appetites, and hardly ever stop feeding all day long. The consequence is, of course, that they grow very quickly; and in a few days' time they find that their jackets are much too tight for them. Then a most curious thing happens. Their skins split right down the back, and they wriggle and twist about, and rub themselves against the surrounding objects, till at last they manage to creep out of them altogether and appear in new ones, which had been gradually forming underneath the old!

Wouldn't it be nice if we could get new suits of clothes, or new frocks, as easily as this?

As soon as their change of garments is over, the little caterpillars begin to feed again, as hungrily as before. But after about a week their new skins are too tight for them, and they have to change them again! This very often happens six or seven times before they are fully fed. But at last they stop eating, throw off their skins once more, and appear as chrysalids.

You may often find these chrysalids on fences and walls, and also on the stems and leaves of bushes and low plants. Sometimes they are suspended by the tips of their tails from little silken pads, which the caterpillars spin for that purpose; and sometimes they are held upright by silken belts round the middle of their bodies. They cannot see, for they have no eyes; and they cannot eat, for they have no mouths; and of course they cannot move about. All that they can do, if you touch them, is just to wriggle their tails from side to side. And there they remain, sometimes for weeks and sometimes for months, till the time comes for the perfect butter-flies to make their appearance.

Then, one day, the skins of the chrysalids split open, and out creep the butterflies. But if you were to see them now you would never guess what they were, for their wings are so tiny, and so crumpled up, that you can hardly see them. They climb up to some firm foothold, however, and then remain perfectly still; and by slow degrees the creases straighten out, and the wings become larger and larger, and stronger and stronger, till at last they reach their full size and strength, and the butterflies, perfect at last, are able to fly away.

That is the "life-history" of a butterfly; and moths are developed in just the same way, except that very often their caterpillars spin silken cells, which we call "cocoons," and turn to chrysalids inside them. And the chrysalids of moths, re-member, are often known as "pupæ."

Then there are one or two other things about these insects that I should like to tell you. One is that their wings are covered all over with very tiny scales.

Of course you know that if you catch a butterfly, and let it go again, your fingers are covered with a kind of mealy dust. And if you look at a little of this dust through a microscope you will find that it is made up of thousands and thousands of the smallest possible scales, all most beautifully chiselled and sculptured, and each with a slender little stalk at the base. And if you look at a piece of the butterfly's wings through the microscope, you will see that these scales are arranged upon it in rows, which overlap one another just like the slates on the roof of a house.

All the colour of a butterfly's wing is in these scales, and if you rub them off you will find that the wing itself is as transparent as that of a bluebottle-fly or a bee.

Then a great many butterflies and moths have a "trunk" or "proboscis" coiled up underneath the head. This is really a long tube, and when the insects are hungry they poke it down into a flower, and suck up the nectar through it. You can see this trunk quite easily if you look sideways at such a butterfly as a "scarlet admiral" or a "peacock."

Then there is just one thing more.

No doubt you would like to know how to tell butterflies from moths. Well, just look at their feelers or "antennæ," as they are often called. You will see that those of butterflies are thickened at the very tips, while those of moths are not. Besides this, the body of a butterfly is nipped in at the middle much more than that of a moth. And when a butterfly is at rest it always folds its wings together over its back, while moths nearly always spread them out, or allow them to hang down, or wrap them round their bodies.

THEODORE WOOD.

LIST OF PLATES

BUTTERFLIES AND MOTHS

PART I

BUTTERFLIES

PLATE I

THE SILVER-WASHED FRITILLARY (1)

THE Fritillaries are handsome golden-brown butterflies, with black blotches and streaks on the upper surface of all the wings, and a number of beautiful silvery spots upon the lower surface of the hinder ones. Nine different kinds are found in Great Britain, but one of these— the "Queen of Spain"—is very rare indeed, and several others are very "local"; that is, they are only found in a few places, so that you are not likely ever to see them. But the Silver-washed Fritillary is common in almost every large wood. You may see it flying about on any warm sunny day in July and the early part of August. And it is very fond indeed of resting with out-spread wings on bramble blossoms, while it eagerly sucks up their sweet juices.

The caterpillar of this beautiful butterfly feeds upon violet leaves. It is rather a curious-looking

A

creature, for it is covered all over with thorny spikes, two of which, placed just behind the head, are a good deal longer than the others. In colour it is black, with yellow lines along the back and sides. About the end of May it hangs itself up by its tail to the stem of a bramble-bush, or some other low shrub, and turns into a fat, humpy, grey chrysalis, spotted all over with silver and gold.

PLATE I

THE PEARL-BORDERED FRITILLARY (2)

This butterfly is only about half as big as the "silver-washed fritillary," for its wings hardly ever measure more than an inch and three-quarters across. It is very common indeed in woods, where you may see it flitting about in almost every open space, first in May, and then again in August. Sometimes, too, you may notice it flying along a hedgerow by the roadside. The caterpillar, which feeds upon the leaves of the dog-violet, is black, with white dots and lines, and the chrysalis is greyish-brown, with paler spots upon the sides.

There is another fritillary, called the "Small Pearl-bordered," which is very much like this butterfly. But you can easily tell the one from the other. All that you have to do is to look at the lower surface of the hind wings. For in the

PLATE II

1

2

1. Small Tortoise-shell
2. Large Tortoise-shell

Pearl-bordered Fritillary there are only nine silvery spots on these wings, while in the small pearl-bordered there are no fewer than seventeen.

This butterfly also lives in woods, and the two may often be seen flying about together.

PLATE II

THE SMALL TORTOISESHELL (1)

This is one of the very commonest of all our British butterflies, and you may see it in almost any month of the year, for it first of all appears early in July, and remains on the wing till about the middle of October. Then it seeks some retired nook, and falls fast asleep until April or the beginning of May, when it leaves its retreat and returns to active life for four or five weeks more. And even in the middle of winter a warmer day than usual will often wake it up for an hour or two from its long slumber, and you may see it flying about, and evidently enjoying the sunshine.

If you want to find the caterpillars of this pretty butterfly, you must look for them on nettle leaves, where you may often see them feeding together in batches of seventy or eighty. They are grey in colour, with a black line running along the back and brown and yellow stripes along the sides, and are covered all over with short,

stiff, bristly hairs.   When they have reached their
full size they wander away from their food-plants,
hang themselves up with their heads downwards
from a twig, or the side of a wall or a paling,
and turn into spiky brown chrysalids, which are
covered almost all over with shining golden spots.

PLATE II

THE LARGE TORTOISESHELL (2)

As a rule, you can easily tell this butterfly from
the last by its size, for it is generally nearly half
as big again.   But just now and then a Large
Tortoiseshell is no bigger than a "small tortoise-
shell," and then it is not always easy to distinguish
the one from the other.   So remember that a
Large Tortoiseshell never has any white spots
upon its wings at all, while the "small tortoise-
shell" always has two, one of which is placed close
to the tip of each of the front pair.

Large Tortoiseshells are not nearly so common
as small ones, but in some years they are much
more plentiful than in others.   They appear in
July or August, sleep all through the winter,
and then fly about again during April and May.
The caterpillars generally feed upon the leaves
of elms, though they will also eat those of willow
and apple and pear trees.   They are brown in
colour, with a broad black stripe along each side,

PLATE III

1

2

3

1. Peacock Butterfly   2. Peacock Caterpillar
3. Red Admiral Butterfly

and are covered with thorny black bristles. About the middle of June they turn into flesh-coloured chrysalids, marked with a number of bright golden spots, which you may sometimes find hanging by their tails on tree-trunks and park palings.

PLATE III

THE PEACOCK (1 and 2)

You cannot possibly mistake this beautiful insect for any other British butterfly, for on each of its four wings it has a large eye-like spot, very much like the markings on the tail of a peacock. But the under-side of the wings is quite differently coloured. It is almost as black as charcoal. And the consequence is that when the butterfly sits on the trunk of a tree, with its wings folded over its back, you cannot possibly see it unless you look at it sideways.

Peacock butterflies are very common in August and September, and again in spring, after they have passed through their long winter sleep. They are very fond of sitting on thistle blossoms when the sun is shining, with their wings widely spread. And you may often see them resting on ivy bloom, or sipping the sweet juices of over-ripe plums. During the winter they hide away in outhouses, and sheds, and faggot-stacks. The caterpillars, which feed in large companies on nettle leaves, are black in colour, sprinkled with little white dots, and are quite as thorny as those of the two tortoiseshells. Look for them in June and July. The chrysalids are green, with their heads and bodies rather brighter than their tails, and with a number of gold spots.

PLATE III

THE RED ADMIRAL (3)

I really think that this is the very handsomest of all our British butterflies; for its wings are of the glossiest possible black above, with spots of the purest possible white, and streaks of the brightest possible scarlet. And on their lower surface so many different tints of grey and pink and brown and red are mingled together that I cannot possibly describe them. All that I can do is to advise you to try to catch one of these butterflies and look at it for yourself; and if you do, I am quite sure that you will say that you have never seen a more beautiful insect.

Red Admiral butterflies are nearly always very common from August till October, and again in April and May, and are quite as fond of ivy bloom and the juices of ripe fruits as peacocks. On almost any warm sunny day you may see them flying about in gardens, or on the borders of woods. Their thorny caterpillars, which are

PLATE IV

2

1

1. Painted Lady
2. Marbled White

yellowish-grey in colour with black markings, and with light yellow lines on each side, may be found feeding on nettle leaves, though not in large companies like those of peacocks and small tortoiseshells. The chrysalids are brown, with gold spots.

PLATE IV

THE PAINTED LADY (1)

In days of old this was not at all a common insect. But in the year 1877 a vast swarm of Painted Ladies came flying across the Straits of Dover, and spread to almost all parts of England. And since then this pretty butterfly has been a good deal more plentiful. But it is much commoner in some years than it is in others. If you want to find it, the very best place to look is a field of red clover in full blossom. The next best place is a field of lucerne. And the next best place to that is a good steep railway bank covered with flowers. But you may often see it resting on thistles and teasels with peacocks and small tortoiseshells.

The caterpillar of this pretty butterfly feeds upon thistle leaves; and for the first fortnight of its life it lives in a sort of little chamber, which it makes by fastening the tips of several leaves together by means of silken threads. It is covered all over with thorny bristles and is brown in

colour, with yellow stripes down the back and
sides. If you want to find it, you should look
for it in June. And when it is fully fed it turns
into a brown and grey chrysalis, marked with a
number of silver spots. The butterfly comes out in
August, and lives till the following May.

PLATE IV

THE MARBLED WHITE (2)

Although its colours are only glossy black and
creamy-white, this is one of the prettiest of all our
British butterflies. But it is quite possible to live
all one's life in the country without ever seeing
it, because it is so very "local." In one field,
perhaps, or on one little patch of ground on a
grassy hillside, it may be very common indeed,
and you may often see fifteen or twenty of the
graceful little insects flying about together. And
yet you may hunt for miles and miles in every
direction, and not see a single one anywhere else.

If you ever happen to find the caterpillar of this
butterfly, you can recognise it at once by its
colouring, for it has a pale green body with a
yellow stripe running along each side, and a
reddish head. And besides this there are two
reddish spikes at the end of the body, forming a
sort of projecting tail. It feeds on different kinds
of grasses in September, and then again, after its

PLATE V

1

2

1. Speckled Wood
2. Wall

long winter sleep, in April and May. Look out for the butterfly in July and the early part of August.

PLATE V

THE SPECKLED WOOD (1)

As you walk through a wood on a bright sunny day at the end of April, or in the beginning of May, you may often see a dark brown butterfly marked with a number of paler spots, which flits along just in front of you for some little distance, and then mounts up over your head and flies back the way it came. This is a Speckled Wood butterfly, or Wood Argus, as it is sometimes called. Argus, as perhaps you know, was a heathen god, who was supposed to have a hundred eyes. And his name has been given to the butterfly on account of the row of eye-like spots which runs along the margin of the hinder wings.

The caterpillar of this butterfly, which is a pretty little green creature with a white stripe along each side, and a dark brown one along its back, feeds on different kinds of grass, first in August and September, and then again in March. Before it enters into its long winter sleep it throws off its skin no less than five times and appears in a new one, which has been forming underneath the old coat. And, strange to say, it always eats its own cast skins! The

B

chrysalis is of a beautiful bright green colour, and you may sometimes find it fastened to grass blades growing beneath trees in woods.

PLATE V

THE WALL BUTTERFLY (2)

I think that you must know this butterfly very well indeed by sight, for it is extremely common in all parts of the country. Indeed in May, and again in August, you can hardly walk along a lane, or through a grassy meadow, without seeing it in dozens whenever the sun is shining. It is called the "Wall" butterfly because it is very fond of resting for a moment or two on the top of a roadside wall. But it seems to have very sharp eyes, for if you walk towards the butterfly it is almost sure to fly swiftly away, only to return to the same spot as soon as you have passed by.

Like that of the "speckled wood," the caterpillar of this butterfly is green in colour, and feeds upon different kinds of grasses. But you can always tell it by the fact that it has three pale lines running along its back instead of one dark brown streak, as well as a rather broader one along each side. The chrysalis is bright apple-green, with a few yellowish-white spots, and you may sometimes find it suspended by its tail from a blade of grass.

PLATE VI

1

2

1. Meadow Brown
2. Ringlet

PLATE VI

THE MEADOW-BROWN (1)

In almost all parts of the country, this is the
very commonest of our British butterflies. From
the beginning of June until quite the end of
August you may see it in hundreds and hundreds, flying about in meadows, or along grassy
banks by the roadside. And even on dull, gloomy
days, when all other butterflies are hiding away
in some snug retreat, it flits to and fro just as
gaily as if the sun were shining brightly.

This is one of the butterflies in which the
female is not quite like the male. For instead
of having just a small dark spot with a white
ring round it on each of the front wings, she
has a large black spot with a little white dot
in the middle. And round this is a patch of
tawny yellow, which occupies nearly a quarter
of the whole wing.

The eggs of the Meadow-brown butterfly are
laid on different kinds of grass. When they
hatch, the little caterpillars feed for about ten
days, and then hide away among the roots, where
they remain fast asleep until the following spring.
In colour they are bright green, with a white
stripe on each side, and when they are fully fed
they turn into pale green chrysalids, marked all
over with purple-black spots.

PLATE VI

THE RINGLET (2)

You can easily see why this butterfly is called the Ringlet, for on the lower surface of its wings it has a number of eye-like spots which are generally so close together that they form a sort of chain, made up of several rings. But the odd thing is that these spots vary very much indeed both in size and number. Generally there are eight quite large ones on each side, three on the front wings and five on the hind ones. But sometimes there are nine, and sometimes there are seven; and just now and then there are only three or four very tiny ones, while you may sometimes catch a Ringlet butterfly which has no spots at all. The upper surface of the wings is always dark smoky brown all over, with only a few very faint spots of a lighter colour.

The best place in which to look for Ringlet butterflies is in grassy paths through woods, where it is sometimes very common indeed. The caterpillars, which feed upon different kinds of grass, are very much like those of the "large heath." But they only come out to feed during the night, so that if you want to find them you will have to look for them with a lantern. They are fully fed about the beginning of June, and the butterfly makes its appearance in July.

PLATE VII

2

1

1. Large Heath
2. Small Heath

PLATE VII

THE LARGE HEATH (1)

This butterfly is very nearly as plentiful as the "meadow-brown," and you can hardly walk along a lane or through a meadow without seeing it. The male is rather different from the female, for he is a good deal smaller, and has a band of dark brown running down from just above the middle of the front wings to the centre of the hind margin.

The caterpillar of this butterfly feeds upon couch-grass. It is greenish-grey in colour, with a reddish head, and has two pale lines running along each of its sides, and a dark one along its back. When it has reached its full size it spins a kind of little silken pad upon a blade of grass, from which it hangs itself up with its head downwards. Two days later it throws off its skin and turns into a fat little greenish-white chrysalis, marked with a number of dark streaks and blotches. Look for the caterpillar in May and the early part of June, for the chrysalis at the end of June, and for the butterfly in July and August.

PLATE VII

THE SMALL HEATH (2)

Of course you know this butterfly very well indeed by sight, for it is extremely common everywhere on heaths and downs and in grassy fields and in lanes from the beginning of June until the end of September. You may often see it gambolling about in company with "meadow-browns" and the pretty little blue butterflies, which are generally so common at the same time of the year. It is quite a small insect, for it only measures about an inch and a quarter across the wings; but in Scotland, strange to say, it is generally a good deal larger than it is in England.

The caterpillar of this butterfly is a little apple-green creature, with a darker stripe edged with white running along its back, and another along each of its sides. It feeds upon grass, and when it is fully fed it spins a kind of silken belt round a grass stem, fastens itself to it with its head hanging downwards, and then changes into a bright green chrysalis with a short purple stripe, bordered with white, on each side.

PLATE VIII

1

2

1. Green Hair Streak
2. Purple Hair Streak

PLATE VIII

THE GREEN HAIR-STREAK (1)

The Hair-streaks are pretty little butterflies which you can very easily tell by sight. For, in the first place, they always have a pale streak, or a row of little white dots, scarcely thicker than a hair, running across the lower surface of the wings. That is why they are called "Hair-streaks." And, in the second place, the hind wings have a pair of little tails, something like those of the swallow-tail butterfly, only of course very much smaller.

Five different kinds of these butterflies are found in the British Islands, but only two of them are at all common. For the Green Hair-streak you should look on heaths, in open spaces in woods, on grassy banks by the roadside, and in other places in which brambles grow. You can easily tell it from all the other Hair-streaks by the bright green colour of its lower surface, and also by its small size, for it only measures about an inch across its outspread wings. The caterpillar, which is light green or greenish-yellow in colour, with a row of triangular yellow spots running along each side, feeds on bramble shoots and blossoms. You may find it in July, and the butterfly makes its appearance in May and June, and sometimes again in August.

PLATE VIII

THE PURPLE HAIR-STREAK (2)

This is the commonest of the Hair-streak butter-flies, for there is scarcely a wood in which oak-trees grow in which you may not find it. But it is quite easy to walk through a wood without seeing it, for it nearly always flies at some little height from the ground. And besides this it is very fond of sitting on leaves and basking in the sun, not moving for some little time unless it is disturbed. The male is much handsomer than the female, for the whole upper surface of the wings, except just the margin, is of the richest possible purple, which seems to shine and glisten in the light, while in his mate there is only a purple blotch in the middle of the wings.

The caterpillar of this butterfly is a most odd little creature, and really looks much more like a little fat slug. It is reddish-brown in colour, with a number of black marks upon its back. You may sometimes find it clinging to oak leaves, on which it feeds. When it is fully grown it generally descends to the ground, buries itself just below the surface, and turns into a fat little brown chrysalis, from which the butterfly appears in July.

PLATE IX

1

2

1. Small Copper
2. Common Blue

PLATE IX

THE SMALL COPPER (1)

This is a very pretty little butterfly indeed, for the upper surface of its front wings is of the richest and most glossy reddish-brown, just like the colour of burnished copper, with nine black spots in the middle, and a narrow blackish border. The hind wings are dark brown, with a broad band of copper running along the margin. It is very plentiful indeed, and you may see it in hundreds by the roadside, or on heaths and in waste places, darting to and fro in the hot sunshine, gambolling with the pretty little "blue" butterflies, or resting on the lilac blossoms of scabious plants. And it has no less than three broods in each year, the first appearing in April, the second in June, and the third in August and September.

The caterpillar of this pretty little butterfly is bright green in colour, with a red stripe running along each side, and another along its back. It feeds on the leaves of sorrel plants, and turns into a whitish chrysalis speckled with black and brown.

Perhaps you may wonder why this insect is called the "Small" Copper. The reason is that there used to be a much larger butterfly, which was very much like it, and which was called the "Large Copper." But this has not been taken for a great many years.

C

PLATE IX

THE COMMON BLUE (2)

Everybody knows the pretty little " Blue " butter-flies, which one sees playing about in such numbers in meadows and by grassy roadsides, all through the summer and the early part of the autumn. But there are several different kinds of these insects, and that which one gener-ally sees is the Common Blue. The male and the female are not quite alike, for the wings of the male are lilac blue all over, while those of the female are much browner, with a row of orange spots running along the hind margin. And the under surface of the male is grey, while that of the female is brown. But, strange to say, " Blues " are sometimes found with the colouring of the male on the wings of one side, and that of the female on those of the other!

The caterpillar of this pretty little butterfly is rather hairy, and is bright green in colour, with a dark stripe running along the back, and a row of little white spots on each side. It feeds on bird's-foot trefoil, rest-harrow, and other low plants, and turns into a small green chrysalis tinged with brown.

PLATE X

1

2

1. Brown Argus
2. Clifton Blue

PLATE X

THE BROWN ARGUS (1)

Although this pretty little butterfly belongs to the family of the "blues," it has no trace of blue in its colouring at all, but is dark brown above, with a row of orange spots along the margin of both the front and the hind wings, and either grey or reddish-brown below. It is very common in most places, and more especially on chalky downs, where you may often see it gambolling about in company with two or three "common blues." And you may also see it flitting about in almost any meadow, just when the hay is ready for cutting. It appears twice in the year, first in May, and then again in August.

In shape, the caterpillar of this butterfly is rather like a fat little slug. It is covered with short white hairs, and is green in colour, with a dark brown stripe along the back, and a narrow pink streak on either side. You may sometimes find it feeding upon the leaves of the hemlock, stork's-bill, and sun-cistus. And when it has finished growing it turns into a little green chrysalis with a deep pink stripe on each side.

PLATE X

THE CLIFTON BLUE (2)

This is one of the loveliest of all our British butterflies, for the upper side of the wings of the male is of the brightest and most vivid blue, like that of the sky on a glorious summer's day, with a white line running along the front margin, and a black line along the hind one. The female, however, is not nearly so handsome, her wings being smoky brown all over, with only just a few blue scales on the parts nearest to the body. The lower surface of the wings, both in the male and the female, is greyish-brown, with a number of black spots edged with white.

If you want to see this beautiful butterfly, you must hunt for it either in May or in August on the chalky downs in the south of England, and in the Isle of Wight. But it is one of the "local" butterflies, and although you may find it quite commonly in one or two places, you may search for it elsewhere for years, and yet never meet with it at all.

The caterpillar of the Clifton Blue, or "Adonis Blue," as it is sometimes called, is green, with yellow streaks. It feeds on trefoils and vetches, and other low plants.

PLATE XI

2

1

1. Chalkhill Blue
2. Little Blue

PLATE XI

THE CHALK-HILL BLUE (1)

You cannot possibly mistake the male of this butterfly for any other insect, for the upper surface of both its front and hind wings is of the most beautiful silvery greenish-blue colour, shading off into a blackish band along the hind border. In fact, as a great naturalist once said, it always makes one think of a bright moonlight night, while the "Clifton blue" reminds one of the sky on a clear summer's day. But the female is so exactly like that of the "Clifton blue" that it is hardly possible to tell the one from the other.

This lovely butterfly is hardly ever found except on chalky downs, and is commonest in the south of England. It flies in July and August. If you want to find the caterpillar, you must look for it in May and the early part of June. It feeds upon bird's-foot trefoil and kidney-vetch, and looks rather like a fat little green woodlouse, with six yellow stripes upon its back and sides; and if you look at these stripes closely, you will see that they are really made of rows of tiny yellow spots. About the middle of June it fastens itself to the stem of its food-plant by spinning a silken band round its body, and then turns into a greenish-brown chrysalis.

PLATE XI

THE LITTLE BLUE (2)

This is a very tiny insect indeed. In fact, it is by far the smallest of all our British butterflies, and you might easily pass it by, over and over again, without noticing it, for it is not at all brightly coloured. The female is dark brown above, without any orange spots on the hind wings, and even the male has only a faint tinge of blue in the middle of his wings. Underneath, both male and female are plain greyish-drab, with rows of tiny black spots enclosed in whitish rings. So you will have to look for it very carefully indeed if you want to see it. It is double-brooded— that is, it makes its appearance twice in the year, first in May, and then again in August. And you may see it flying about in meadows and on heaths, more especially in chalky or lime- stone districts.

The caterpillar of this odd little butterfly, like that of the chalk-hill blue, is shaped like a tiny woodlouse, and is green in colour, with an orange stripe running along its back, and another on each side. It feeds upon kidney- vetch, or "woundwort," as it is sometimes called, and turns into a little yellow chrysalis, marked with three rows of black spots.

This butterfly is sometimes known as the Bed- ford Blue.

PLATE XII

1

2

1. Azure Blue
2. Brimstone

PLATE XII

THE AZURE BLUE (1)

I do not know why this pretty butterfly is called the "Azure" Blue; for azure is a very bright blue indeed, and yet the insect is not nearly so brilliantly coloured as the Clifton blue. Indeed, it is lilac in colour, rather than blue. But sometimes it is called the "Holly Blue," and that is a very much better name for it; for one often sees it flying along by the side of holly hedges, while the caterpillar feeds upon holly blossoms, as well as upon those of buckthorn and ivy. It is the first of all the "blues" to appear in the spring, and you may sometimes see it even in April. And generally there is another brood towards the end of the summer.

You can easily tell the female of this butterfly from the male, for her front wings have a broad black border, while that on the wings of her mate is very narrow indeed. The caterpillar is greenish-yellow in colour, with a black head and black legs, and a bright green streak running along the middle of the back. When it has reached its full size it turns into a small yellowish-brown chrysalis.

PLATE XII

THE BRIMSTONE BUTTERFLY (2)

This very handsome insect is common in almost all parts of the country, and is one of the very first butterflies to be seen in the spring. On warm, sunny days in March, or even in February, you may often meet with it. For it is one of those butterflies which "hibernate"—that is, it comes out of the chrysalis in the summer or early autumn, and then sleeps all through the winter in some snug retreat, from which it is always ready to come out for an hour or two when the weather is a little warmer and finer than usual.

The male Brimstone is a good deal handsomer than the female, for his wings are of a bright daffodil colour, while those of his mate are pale greenish-yellow. The caterpillar feeds on the young leaves of buckthorn bushes, and is dull green in colour, sprinkled all over with tiny black spots, from each of which sprouts a slender white bristle, and the chrysalis, which is fastened by a silken belt round its body to a twig of the food-plant, is bright apple-green marked with yellow and purple-brown.

PLATE XIII

1. Clouded Yellow
2. Pale Clouded

PLATE XIII

THE CLOUDED YELLOW (1)

I wonder if you have ever seen this very hand-some butterfly alive. Very likely you have not, for although just now and then it is very common indeed, it nearly always becomes quite scarce for several years afterwards, and you may look for it summer after summer without seeing it at all. It makes its appearance in August and September, and the best places in which to look for it are clover and lucerne fields near the seaside. But it is also very fond of flying about on railway banks; and if you try to chase it *there* you will find that you will have to run very hard indeed if you want to catch it! In fact, one butterfly collector used to say that it was of no use trying to do so unless one wore a pair of seven-leagued boots!

The caterpillar of the Clouded Yellow butterfly is of a bright grass-green colour, with a white line on each side, marked with yellow and orange. It feeds on the leaves of lucerne, trefoils, and clover in June and July, and then changes into a green chrysalis shaped something like that of a "large white," with a pale yellow stripe on each side, and a number of black and reddish-brown spots.

D

PLATE XIII

THE PALE CLOUDED YELLOW (2)

Sometimes this butterfly is known as the Clouded Sulphur. It appears in the same places, and at the same time of the year, as the "clouded yellow," but is hardly ever quite as common. Generally, indeed, you may see ten or twelve "clouded yellows" to one Pale Clouded Yellow. You can easily tell it by its much paler colour, for its wings are quite light yellow instead of rich orange, while sometimes one meets with a Pale Clouded Yellow which is really almost white. And, besides that, the black border of the upper wings, instead of being nearly the same width all the way along, is very broad at the top and very narrow at the bottom, while even in the male it is marked with several yellow spots.

This pretty butterfly is quite a seaside insect, and sometimes it may be seen fluttering over the waves a long way out from the shore. Indeed, there seems to be very little doubt that now and then it flies right across the Straits of Dover, and reaches this country from France!

The caterpillar of the Pale Clouded Yellow is olive-green in colour, sprinkled with black dots, and with two yellow lines along its back and another on each side. It feeds on clovers and trefoils.

PLATE XIV

1

2

1 Swallow-tail
2 Swallow-tail Caterpillar

PLATE XIV

THE SWALLOW-TAIL (1 and 2)

This is the finest of all our British butterflies, and a most beautiful creature it is as it flits to and fro in the sunshine. But I am afraid that you are not very likely to see it alive, for it is only found in the fens of Norfolk and Cambridgeshire, while even there it is not as common as it used to be. But if ever you spend a summer holiday in the Norfolk Broads you may, perhaps, see one of these lovely butterflies flying swiftly past you.

The caterpillar is almost as handsome as the butterfly. It is bright green in colour, with velvety-black rings, which are spotted with red. And just behind its head it has an odd little forked organ, from which it pours out a drop of liquid when it is frightened. This liquid has a very nasty smell, and no doubt it prevents birds from feeding upon the caterpillar.

This caterpillar feeds upon hog's fennel, wild carrot, and marsh milk-parsley. When it has reached its full size it climbs up the stem of a reed, fastens itself to it by spinning a kind of silken belt round its body, and turns into a yellowish-green chrysalis, from which the butter-fly appears during the following summer.

PLATE XV

THE ORANGE-TIP (1 and 2)

You must often have noticed this very pretty insect flying about in the spring, for it is quite common in almost all parts of the country. And you cannot possibly mistake the male for any other butterfly, because of the large patch of orange-yellow at the tips of the front wings. But the female is without this orange patch, so that you might easily take her for one of the small white butterflies. If you can look at her closely, however, you will notice that in the middle of her front wings she has a small black spot shaped just like the crescent moon, and that the lower surface of her hind wings is marbled with yellowish-green.

The caterpillar of this pretty butterfly feeds upon cuckoo-flower, or "lady's smock," as it is sometimes called, and also upon hedge garlic, tower mustard, and yellow rocket. In colour it is green, with a white stripe running along each side of its body. When it is fully fed it fastens itself by a silken belt to the stem of its food-plant, and turns into a long, slender, greenish-brown chrysalis, shaped like a bow, from which the butterfly appears in the following May.

PLATE XV

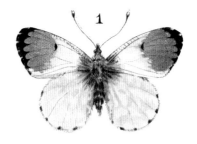

1. Orange Tip, male
2. Orange Tip, female

PLATE XVI

THE LARGE WHITE (1 and 2)

This is a very common butterfly indeed, and
even in towns you may often see it flying about.
Indeed it is much too common, for its caterpillars
feed upon the leaves of cabbages and cauliflowers,
to which they sometimes do most terrible mischief.
I dare say that you have seen these plants so
stripped by the caterpillars of "Garden Whites,"
as these butterflies are often called, that they
look just like skeletons, only the mid-ribs and
the veins being left remaining. And in some
summers these caterpillars are so plentiful that
hardly a single cabbage or cauliflower escapes.

You can easily recognise this butterfly by its
size; and you can tell the female from the male
by the two black spots and the narrow black
streak upon her front wings. The caterpillar is
green in colour, shaded on each side with yellow,
and is dotted all over with tiny black spots, from
each of which springs a hair. When it has
reached its full size it leaves its food-plant,
fastens itself to a wall, or a fence, or a door-post,
or the trunk of a tree, and turns into a rather stout
bluish-white chrysalis, sprinkled with blackish
spots. The butterfly may be seen in May, and
again in August.

PLATE XVI

THE SMALL WHITE (3 and 4)

This butterfly is even commoner than the last. Indeed, two butterflies out of every three which you see on a warm summer's day are almost sure to be Small Whites, and they are always very plentiful indeed in gardens, where their caterpillars often do a great deal of mischief. You can easily tell them from the caterpillars of the "large white," for they are pale green in colour, with a yellow line running down the middle of the back, and a dotted line of the same colour on either side. And instead of having short, stiff hairs all over their bodies, they are covered with a kind of very soft down. They, too, feed upon cabbages and cauliflowers, but instead of eating away the outer leaves only, like those of the "large white," they bore their way right into the very heart of the plants, and often quite spoil them for use as human food. Very often, too, you may find them feeding on the leaves of nasturtiums, and also on those of mignonette.

This butterfly, like the last, appears in the early spring, and again in summer, and you can tell the female from the male by the two black spots upon her front wings. The chrysalis is sometimes green in colour, and sometimes yellow, and sometimes light or reddish-brown.

PLATE XVI

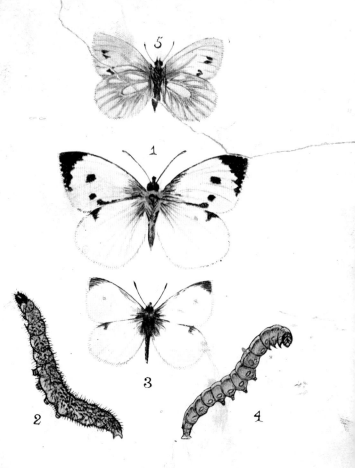

1. Large White
3. Small White
5. Green-veined White, under-side

2. Large White Caterpillar
4. Small White Caterpillar

PLATE XVI

THE GREEN-VEINED WHITE (5)

From a little distance you might very easily mistake this butterfly for a "small white"; for it is of just the same size, and the upper surface of its wings is marked in almost exactly the same way. But if you happen to see it sitting with its wings closed, you will notice at once that the veins on the lower surface of the hinder pair are streaked with green or grey. It is not quite as common as the "small white," but you may see it flying about in almost any part of the country in May, and again in August.

This butterfly lays its eggs on hedge-garlic, and also on winter-cress and sometimes on water-cress. They are most beautiful little objects if you look at them through a microscope, for they are shaped just like little tiny sugar-loaves, with ridges running down them from the top to the bottom, and smaller ridges crosswise between them. The caterpillars which hatch out of them are darker green above and lighter green below, with a row of little black spots on either side, each of which is enclosed in a yellow ring; and the chrysalis is green, sprinkled all over with the tiniest possible black spots.

PLATE XVII

THE GRIZZLED SKIPPER (1)

Skipper butterflies are common enough in almost all parts of the country; yet very few people ever seem to notice them. The reason is that they hardly look like butterflies at all. They look much more like little grey or brown moths. Yet they are really butterflies, for if you look at them closely you will see that their feelers have little knobs at the tips. And that is one of the marks of a butterfly.

It is very easy to see why these little insects are called "Skippers," for they seem to *skip* from flower to flower in a manner quite unlike the flight of any other butterfly. And the Grizzled Skipper is one of the commonest of them all. You may see it darting about in May, and again in August, in open grassy places in woods. But it only seems to live for a short time, so that although it may be flying about in numbers one day, two or three days later it will have quite disappeared. The caterpillar is sometimes green and sometimes brown in colour, with paler lines along its back and sides. It feeds for a few weeks on bramble leaves, and then turns into a dull white chrysalis spotted with black.

PLATE XVII

1. Grizzled Skipper
3. Large Skipper

2. Dingy Skipper
4. Small Skipper

PLATE XVII

THE DINGY SKIPPER (2)

This little butterfly certainly deserves its name. One cannot call it a pretty insect, for it is just dull, dingy brown all over, with just a faint grey band running across the middle of the wings. So unless you look very carefully for it you are not likely to see it. It does not live in woods, like the "grizzled skipper," but flies about on flowery chalk banks in the sunshine, first in May, and then again in August. And sometimes you may see it in numbers in an old chalk-pit, never resting on one flower for more than a very few moments, but skipping about in the most active way from one blossom to another.

The caterpillar of this little butterfly feeds on the bird's-foot trefoil, that low plant with yellow flowers which grows so commonly on chalky banks. If you should ever happen to find this caterpillar you can tell it at once by its colour, which is pale green, with two yellow stripes running along each side of the body, and over each stripe is a row of little black dots. When it has finished growing it turns into a fat and rather bunchy little chrysalis, which is dull green in front and rosy-red behind.

PLATE XVII

THE LARGE SKIPPER (3)

The Large Skipper is one of the commonest of all these queer little butterflies, and you may see it in dozens and dozens, skipping actively about from flower to flower on grassy banks by the roadside, and in open places in woods. The male is not quite like the female, for he has a rather large streak of dark brown running across his front wings, which look as if they had been scorched down the middle. And the body of the female is so very stout that she certainly looks much more like a moth than a butterfly.

If you want to find the caterpillar of this insect you must look for it on different kinds of meadow-grass. It has a big brown head and a dull green body, with a dark line running along the back dotted with black. And underneath, on the hinder part of its body, it has a number of white spots. When it is fully grown it fastens three or four grass-stems together by means of silken threads, and then turns to a rather long and thin chrysalis of a pale brown colour between them. Look out for the butterfly on bright sunny days in May, and again in August.

PLATE XVIII

1

2

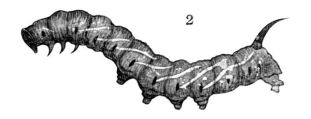

1. Eyed Hawk
2. Eyed Hawk Caterpillar

PLATE XVII

THE SMALL SKIPPER (4)

This queer little butterfly, which is about half the size of the "large skipper," is very nearly as common. But it only makes its appearance once in the year instead of twice, generally about the middle of July. The best places in which to look for it are grassy banks by the sides of lanes and open places in woods. But it is so small that unless you look very carefully you will most likely pass it by. The male butterfly is not quite like the female, for he has a thin black line running along the middle of his front wings.

This butterfly lays its eggs on different kinds of grass, and when they hatch, the little caterpillars feed for a few weeks, and then find their way into some snug retreat, in which they sleep all through the autumn and winter. Early in the spring they come out from their hiding-places and begin to feed again; and by about the beginning of June they are ready to turn into chrysalids. If ever you should happen to find them you may know them at once, for they are green in colour, with six white stripes running all the way along their bodies. And besides this they are quite fat in the middle, and quite thin at the head and the tail.

MOTHS

PLATE XVIII

THE EYED HAWK MOTH (1 and 2)

The "hawk moths" are so called because their flight is so swift and strong, very much like that of a hawk. Most of them come out soon after sunset on warm summer evenings, and you may often see them hovering in front of such flowers as honeysuckle, and verbenas, and petunias, with their long trunks poked deeply into the blossoms in order that they may suck up their sweet juices. But if you move in the very least they dart away at once, so quickly that you cannot even tell in which direction they have gone.

The Eyed Hawk is one of the most beautiful of these grand moths. You can easily see why its name was given to it, for the big spot on each of its hind-wings is very much like the "eyes" on a peacock's tail. The caterpillar is pale green in colour, with a very rough skin, and with seven white stripes on each side of its body, and a curved blue horn upon its tail. You may often find it feeding on the leaves of

PLATE XIX

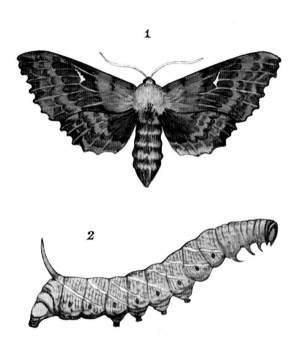

1. Poplar Hawk
2. Poplar Hawk Caterpillar

apple trees in August and September. It then buries itself in the ground below, and changes to a shiny reddish-brown chrysalis, from which the moth makes its appearance early in the following June.

PLATE XIX

THE POPLAR HAWK (1 and 2)

This is a very handsome moth indeed, which makes its appearance about the end of May or the beginning of June, when you may often see it resting on fences, or on the trunks of poplar trees. After dark, too, you may sometimes see it flying round and round street lamps; and just now and then it will come into a lighted room through an open window. And in August and the early part of September you may find the caterpillar, which feeds on the leaves of poplar trees, and also on those of willows and laurus-tinus. It grows to a length of nearly three inches, and is green in colour, sprinkled with yellow. And you can always tell it from that of any other hawk moth by the seven yellow and white stripes on its sides, and also by the yellow horn on its tail. About the middle of September it reaches its full size, and then burrows down into the ground at the roots of the tree on which it has been feeding, and turns to a rough brown chrysalis with a short spike at the end of its body, which always looks as if it had been dipped into very muddy water, and dried without being wiped!

PLATE XX

THE LIME HAWK (1 and 2)

Although it is not quite so large, this is an even handsomer moth than the "poplar hawk," for its wings are tinted with the most beautiful shades of green and brown and brownish-yellow. When it is resting on a fence or a tree-trunk, indeed, it looks very much like a folded leaf, and you might easily pass it by without noticing it. The caterpillar feeds on the leaves of quite a number of trees, such as lime, and elm, and beech, and birch, and oak. But it much prefers the two first of these, on which you may find it during August and the early part of September. It is green in colour, sprinkled with tiny yellow dots, and has seven yellow stripes on each side, bordered with red. The horn at the end of the body is blue or green above and yellow beneath, and underneath it is a sort of flat horny plate, which is purple in colour, with a yellow edge. About the second week in September it buries itself in the ground and turns to a reddish-brown chrysalis with a spiky tail, out of which the moth hatches towards the end of the following May.

PLATE XX

1

2

1. Lime Hawk
2. Lime Hawk Caterpillar

PLATE XXI

1. Death's Head
2. Death's Head Caterpillar

PLATE XXI

THE DEATH'S HEAD HAWK (1 and 2)

This is the largest of all the British hawk moths, for its outspread wings often measure as much as five inches from tip to tip. You cannot possibly mistake it for any other insect, for on its back it has a patch of short yellow hair which looks just like a skull. That is why it is called the "Death's Head." If you want to find the caterpillar you should look for it in potato fields in the month of August. It is a great yellow creature, four or even five inches in length, with seven blue stripes on each side, and a yellow horn on its tail. And if you meet with it, and pick it up, you will be surprised to find that it can squeak quite loudly! Stranger still, the chrysalis can squeak too, and so can the moth! Indeed, if you pick up a Death's Head Hawk Moth it will go on squeaking very much like a mouse all the time that you hold it in your hand!

The caterpillar of this grand moth feeds chiefly on potato leaves, but is sometimes found on jessamine and buckthorn. When it is fully fed it buries itself eight or ten inches deep in the ground, and turns into a huge reddish-brown chrysalis, from which the moth generally hatches out in October.

PLATE XXII

THE PRIVET HAWK (1 and 2)

Wherever privet bushes grow you may expect to find this handsome insect, which is sometimes very nearly as large as the "death's head." One does not very often see the perfect moth, however, for it only flies by night, and contrives to hide itself away in some secure retreat during the hours of daylight. But sometimes you may see it at dusk hovering in front of petunia blossoms, and sucking up their sweet juices through its long slender trunk. You may find the caterpillar, however, in almost every garden if you look for it during August or the early part of September. It is a most beautiful creature, of the brightest apple-green colour, with seven purple stripes on either side, each of which is edged with yellow below. And on its tail is a glossy black horn with a yellow base. It feeds chiefly on the leaves of privet, but you may sometimes find it on those of lilac and elder. When it reaches its full size it buries itself in the ground and turns into a big reddish-brown chrysalis, from which the moth hatches out about midsummer in the following year.

PLATE XXII

1

2

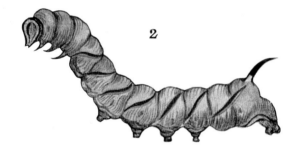

1. Privet Hawk
2. Privet Hawk Caterpillar

PLATE XXIII

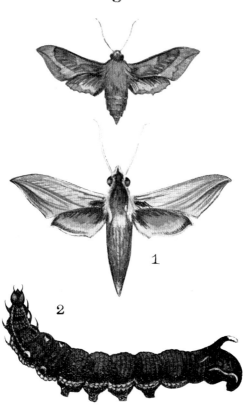

1. Elephant Hawk   2. Elephant Hawk Caterpillar
3. Small Elephant Hawk

PLATE XXIII

THE ELEPHANT HAWK (1 and 2)

If you were only to see this moth itself, and not its caterpillar, you would be quite sure to wonder why it should ever have been called the "Elephant" Hawk. For it is not in the least like an elephant in any way at all. But the moment you look at the caterpillar you understand why this name was given to it; for the front part of its body is so long and slender that it really does remind one rather of an elephant's trunk. And just behind it, on each side, is a big round spot which looks like an eye.

If you want to find this curious caterpillar you should look for it in August on willow-herb and bedstraw plants which grow on the banks of ditches and streams. Now and then, too, you may find it feeding on fuchsias in gardens. It is sometimes green in colour, and sometimes dull grey or brown, and the horn at the end of its body is black, with a white tip. The moth, as you will see by its picture, is a very pretty one indeed, and you may see it hovering in front of flowers at dusk in May and June.

F

PLATE XXIII

THE SMALL ELEPHANT HAWK (3)

This is a much smaller insect than the last,
for its wings only measure about an inch and
three-quarters from tip to tip when they are fully
spread out. But it is one of the prettiest of all
our British moths, with a rose-coloured body,
and greenish-yellow wings marked with rose-
coloured bands and spots. It is not at all
uncommon, and if you want to see it you can
very easily do so. All that you have to do is to
stand at dusk on a warm evening in June in
front of a honeysuckle bush, and then to remain
perfectly still. After a few minutes you are
almost sure to see a shadowy form hovering in
front of one of the blossoms. This is a Small
Elephant Hawk; and if you catch it, and wait
for a little while, another one is almost sure to
make its appearance in a very few minutes.

The caterpillar of this moth is something like
that of the "large elephant hawk," but has three
eye-like spots on each side of its body, and no
horn upon its tail. It feeds upon bedstraw, and
is generally found in places where the soil is
chalky.

PLATE XXIV

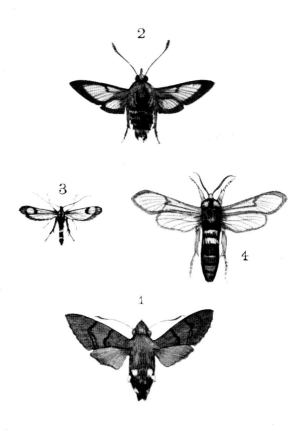

1. Humming Bird Hawk
2. Bee Hawk
3. Currant Clearwing
4. Hornet Clearwing

PLATE XXIV

THE HUMMING-BIRD HAWK (1)

On a hot summer's day you may often see this
beautiful moth hovering in front of geraniums
and other flowers in the garden, with its long
trunk plunged deeply down into the blossoms in
order to suck up their sweet juices. And if you
stand a few feet away and listen carefully, you
will hear a low humming noise, which is caused
by the rapid movements of the wings. It looks
and sounds, in fact, very much like a humming-
bird, and people who have lived for many years
in hot countries, and have then come to England,
have often found it very difficult to believe that
they were looking at a moth, and not at one of
the beautiful little birds which they had known
so well.

The caterpillar of the Humming-bird Hawk is
greenish-brown, or bluish-green, sprinkled with
tiny white dots, and with a pinkish-white stripe
running along each side of its body. Below this
is another stripe of dull yellow, and at the end
of the body is a blue horn with a yellow tip. It
feeds upon bedstraw, and when it has finished
growing it buries itself just below the surface
of the ground, and then turns into a reddish-
brown chrysalis.

PLATE XXIV

THE BEE HAWK (2)

There are really two "bee hawks," which you can recognise at once by their transparent wings. And as one of them has a narrow black border to its wings, while the other has a broad one, they are called the Narrow-bordered Bee Hawk, and the Broad-bordered Bee Hawk. And really they do look more like very big bumble-bees than moths. They fly by day, like the "humming-bird hawk," and you may sometimes see them hovering in front of rhododendron blossoms on a bright sunny day in May, and darting away at the slightest alarm with almost the speed of light. But they are not very common, and in many parts of the country they are never seen at all.

The caterpillar of the "broad-bordered bee hawk" feeds upon honeysuckle, and that of the "narrow-bordered bee hawk" upon field scabious —that common low plant which looks so much like a rather small thistle. They are both green in colour, dotted with yellowish-white, and with a brown horn at the end of the body. When they have finished growing they spin little silken webs on the surface of the ground, and turn to chrysalids inside them.

PLATE XXIV

THE CURRANT CLEARWING (3)

The "clearwings" are very odd little moths with transparent wings, which have no scales upon them at all, except just on the narrow black borders. The consequence is that they do not look in the least like moths. They look much more like flies, or gnats, or wasps, or hornets. They nearly all come out in June and July, and you may see them resting on leaves in the hot sunshine.

Another curious thing about the "clearwings" is that their caterpillars feed, not upon the leaves of plants and trees, like almost all other caterpillars, but upon the pith of the stems or the twigs, or even upon the solid wood of the trunk or the branches; so it is very difficult indeed to find them. When they are fully fed they turn into chrysalids with rows of tiny hooks along their bodies, by means of which they can wriggle their way backwards and forwards along the burrows which they made when they were caterpillars.

The Currant Clearwing is so called because its caterpillar feeds on the pith in the young shoots of currant bushes. It is very common in almost every kitchen-garden, and sometimes does a good deal of mischief to the currants.

PLATE XXIV

THE HORNET CLEARWING (4)

This is the largest of all the British "clear-wings," and it really does look so very much like a hornet that most people would be quite afraid to meddle with it for fear of being stung. But if ever you should happen to meet with the moth you can tell it from a real hornet quite easily; for if you look closely at it you will see that its body is not smooth and shiny, but is covered all over with close, soft down. The best place to look for it is on the trunks of poplar trees, quite close to the ground, in June and July; for after it comes out of the chrysalis it always sits on the tree-trunk for some little time in order to dry its wings. And you will nearly always find that it is sitting quite close to the burrow which it made when it was a caterpillar, and in which it lived for no less than two whole years.

There is another kind of "hornet clearwing," whose caterpillar feeds in the stems of osiers instead of in the trunks of poplar trees. But it is not at all a common insect, and you are not very likely ever to find it.

PLATE XXV

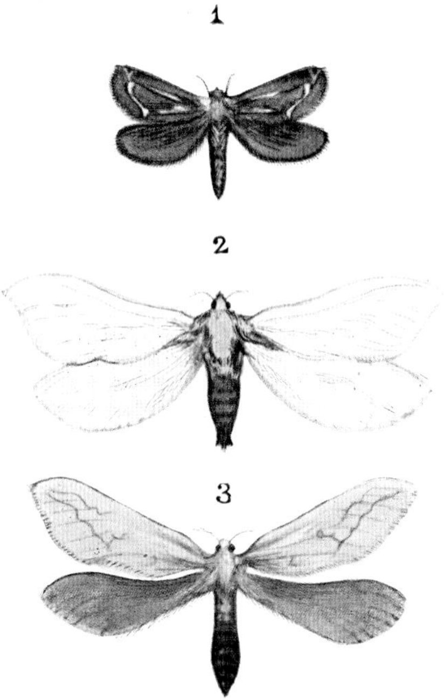

1. Common Swift
2. Ghost Swift, male
3. Ghost Swift, female

PLATE XXV

THE COMMON SWIFT (1)

The "swift" moths owe their name to their rapid flight, for they can all fly very swiftly indeed when they are alarmed. But very often, on a warm summer's evening, you may see them in grassy places in woods *swinging*, as it were, in the air—flying first a foot or so to one side, and then a foot or two to the other side, over and over again, just like the pendulum of a clock. And when they are doing this they do not seem at all ready to take the alarm, so that you can easily catch them.

Five kinds of these moths are found in the British Islands, of which the Common Swift is by far the most plentiful. It lives, not only in woods, but also in lanes and on the borders of fields, and on warm evenings in June you may see it darting swiftly along almost any hedgerow. And if you catch a dozen or so you will find that the males are all spotted and streaked with white, while the females are plain dingy brown all over. And, besides that, you will see that no two of the males are quite alike, some of them having a great many more white markings than the others.

The caterpillar of this moth lives underground, and feeds on the roots of dumb nettles.

PLATE XXV

THE GHOST SWIFT (2 and 3)

That is rather a curious name to give to a moth, isn't it? But the very first time that you notice the male insect flying about on a warm summer's evening you will see why the title was given to it; for it keeps on suddenly appearing and disappearing, over and over again, just as if it had the power of making itself visible or invisible whenever it chose. The fact is that the upper surface of the wings is glossy white, while the lower is dark brown, and that as the insect flies you can see the one and not the other. So every time that the wings are lowered the moth appears; and every time that they are raised it disappears.

The wings of the female, however, are yellowish-brown, with darker markings, so that she is not nearly so ghost-like as her mate. You may sometimes see her flying slowly to and fro in the dusk, and as she does so she keeps on dropping her eggs, which fall to the ground below. After a short time they hatch, and out come a number of little dirty white caterpillars, which burrow down into the soil, and feed on the roots of burdock, stinging nettle, and dumb nettle, and sometimes on those of hops.

PLATE XXVI

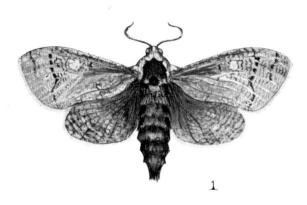

1

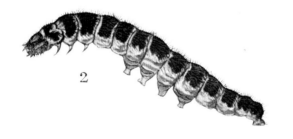

2

1. Goat Moth
2. Goat Caterpillar

PLATE XXVI

THE GOAT MOTH (1 and 2)

Somehow or other, one does not very often see this moth, although it is quite common in almost all parts of the country. But just now and then it flies through an open window into a well-lighted room at night, and then it looks so big as it goes blundering about that one might almost mistake it for a bat.

Nearly everybody sometimes sees the caterpillar, however—a great flesh-coloured creature three or four inches long, with a black head, and a broad band of chocolate-brown running all the way along its back. Like that of the wood leopard, it feeds in the trunks of trees, in which it lives for three whole years; and out from its burrow a dark brown liquid comes oozing, which smells something like the odour of a he-goat. That is why the insect is called the "Goat" Moth. When this caterpillar is fully grown it leaves its burrow, and goes crawling about in search of a convenient place in which to spin its cocoon; and this is the time when one generally sees it. The moth appears in June and July, and you should look for the caterpillar in September.

G

PLATE XXVII

THE WOOD LEOPARD (1)

This is not a very common moth, but it seems rather more plentiful than it used to be, more especially near London. You may sometimes see it resting on the trunks of trees in July and August. Then, if you examine the tree-trunk carefully, you are almost sure to find the entrance to the burrow out of which it came; for the caterpillar of this moth is one of those which feed on the solid wood of trees. The female moth lays her eggs in the crevices of the bark, and as soon as the little caterpillars appear they nibble their way into the trunk with their powerful jaws, and there live for several months, burrowing backwards and forwards, day after day, till sometimes the wood is almost honeycombed with their tunnels. Sometimes they live in oak trees, sometimes in elms, sometimes in beeches, or ashes, or willows. But the wood that they like most of all is that of apple and plum and pear trees; so that the very best place to look for the moth is in an orchard.

If you ever find a Wood Leopard you will notice that its wings are partly transparent. That is because they have fewer scales upon them than those of most moths, so that they look rather as if they had been rubbed.

PLATE XXVII

1. Wood Leopard
2. Green Forester
3. Six Spot Burnet

PLATE XXVII

THE GREEN FORESTER (2)

When one first sees this pretty little insect flitting about in the hot sunshine it is rather difficult to believe that it is really a moth, for it looks a great deal more like a bright green fly. The best places in which to look for it are grassy clearings in woods in which mulleins are growing; for it is very fond indeed of resting on the blossoms of those plants, where its glossy green wings form a most lovely contrast to the yellow petals. On dull days, however, it never flies at all; and even on fine ones, if the sun is clouded over for more than a very few minutes, all the Green Foresters are sure to disappear.

The caterpillar of this moth is shaped exactly like a tiny woodlouse, and its legs are so short that you can only just see its feet projecting from underneath its fat little body. It is dingy green in colour, with a line of black spots running along the middle of its back, and a pale stripe along each side. It feeds on the common sorrel, and when it is fully fed it spins a little silken cocoon among the leaves, and turns to a chrysalis inside it. Look for the caterpillar in May and the early part of June, and for the moth about midsummer.

PLATE XXVII

THE SIX-SPOT BURNET (3)

The "burnets" are most lovely little moths, with glossy blackish-green front wings, marked with bright crimson spots, and crimson hind-wings with dark green borders. Like the "green forester," they fly only in the hot sunshine; but even on dull days you may often see them clinging to grass stems in fields and by the roadside.

Several different kinds of these moths are found in the British Islands, of which the Six-spot Burnet is by far the commonest. On a hot day about the middle of June you may often see it flying about in hundreds. And if you look on the grass stems you are almost sure to find numbers of its odd little cocoons, which are bright yellow in colour, and look just like tiny shuttles with very sharp points. The caterpillars which spin these cocoons, however, feed chiefly on trefoils and clovers. They are dingy yellow in colour, with rather hairy bodies, marked with two rows of small black spots on either side. You may find them towards the end of May, and they spin their cocoons early in June.

PLATE XXVIII

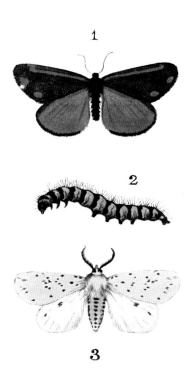

1

2

3

1. Cinnabar
2. Cinnabar Caterpillar
3. White Ermine

PLATE XXVIII

THE CINNABAR (1 and 2)

The Cinnabar Moth is really almost a prettier insect than the "burnets," and it looks most beautiful as you see it slowly flying over the long grass in the hay-fields, or along a bank by the roadside, on a hot midsummer day. For the upper wings are deep olive-brown in colour, with a broad crimson streak and two round crimson spots upon them, while the lower ones are rich crimson with a narrow black margin. And the under surface is coloured just like the upper, except that the crimson tint is just a little bit paler.

This is one of the "local" moths, for while it is very common indeed in some places, it is seldom or never seen in others. You should look for it where ragwort grows, for on that plant the caterpillars feed. They are handsome little creatures, which you cannot possibly mistake for those of any other moth, for they are bright orange in colour, with black rings round their bodies. And sometimes they are so plentiful that they quite strip the ragwort plants of their leaves. When they are fully fed they change into shiny reddish-brown chrysalids on the surface of the ground.

PLATE XXVIII

THE WHITE ERMINE (3)

In most parts of the British Islands this is a very common moth indeed. You may see it resting by day on fences and the trunks of trees, and after dark it will often come flying into a lighted room. Or you may notice it darting round and round street-lamps by night, and doing its very best to burn itself in the dazzling flame. And the caterpillar is even commoner in gardens than that of the "tiger" moth. It is really a sort of small "woolly bear," for its body is covered all over with brown hairs. But you can always tell it from the real "woolly bear" by the pale line which runs along the middle of its back. It will feed on almost any plant in the garden, and is fully grown about the middle of September, when it spins a silken cocoon, and turns into a dark brown chrysalis. The moth appears in June.

There is another kind of "ermine" moth, called the "buff ermine," which is brownish-yellow in colour instead of white. The caterpillar is dingy white, with one white line and two dark ones running along its back, and is covered with pale brown hairs. You may often find it feeding upon dock leaves. The moth is quite as common as the White Ermine, and makes its appearance at the same time of the year.

PLATE XXIX

1. Garden Tiger
3. Cream Spotted Tiger

2. Garden Tiger Caterpillar
4. Cream Spotted Tiger Caterpillar

PLATE XXIX

THE GARDEN TIGER (1 and 2)

Most likely you know the caterpillar of this moth a good deal better than the moth itself; for you may find it in almost any garden feeding on the leaves of hollyhocks and all sorts of other plants, while you can hardly walk along a hedge bank without noticing it upon those of the dumb-nettles. It is called the "woolly bear," because it is covered all over with long brown hairs which look something like the fur of a bear, and when it has finished growing it spins a silken cocoon amongst the herbage, in which a number of these hairs are always entangled.

But although it is so common one does not often see the moth. For it only flies by night, and hides away so cleverly during the day that one very seldom finds it. But sometimes it will fly through an open window into a well-lighted room, or cling to a street-lamp and gaze at the flame for hours together.

A curious fact about this moth is that it varies very much in colour and markings. Indeed, it would not be very difficult to make a small collection of "tiger" moths, no two of which should be quite alike. It appears on the wing in July, and you may find the caterpillar in May and June.

PLATE XXIX

THE CREAM-SPOTTED TIGER (3 and 4)

This is not nearly such a common insect as the "garden tiger." But at the same time it is a good deal commoner than it seems, for it is such a sluggish creature that it very seldom flies, and the consequence is that one hardly ever sees it. It does not vary very much in colour, for the front wings are always black, with eight large creamy-white spots, and the hind-wings are orange-yellow, with six or seven small black spots, and a big black patch near the margin. The body is black in front, with a white blotch on each side, and orange-red behind with a row of black spots down the middle; so the insect is really a very handsome one indeed.

The caterpillar of this moth is quite as woolly as that of the "garden tiger." It is almost black in colour, with a red head and red legs, while the long hairs which cover its body are brown. It feeds upon chickweed in September, and again in April and May, and then spins a silken web, in which it turns to a chrysalis. The moth makes its appearance about the end of June.

PLATE XXX

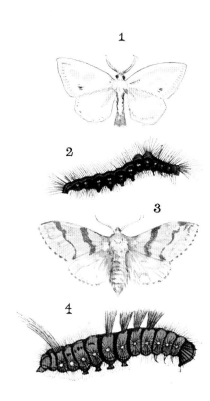

1. Gold Tail
3. Pale Tussock

2. Gold Tail Caterpillar
4. Pale Tussock Caterpillar

PLATE XXX

THE GOLD-TAIL (1 and 2)

Of course you know this pretty insect very well indeed by sight, for it is one of the commonest of all our British moths. You cannot possibly mistake it for any other, because of its snowy white wings and the thick tuft of long yellow hairs at the end of its body, from which it gets its name of "Gold-tail." In the female moth this tuft is very long and thick indeed, and she puts it to a most curious purpose. For when she has laid her eggs she strips off the golden down from her tail and covers them carefully over with it, leaving the tip of her body almost bare!

The caterpillars which hatch out of the eggs are most beautiful little creatures. They are black in colour, with three rows of tiny pimples, so to speak, on each side, from every one of which springs a little tuft of hairs. Those of the upper row are jetty - black; those of the middle row are white; and those of the lower one are bright scarlet. Besides this, there are two scarlet stripes running down the back, and just behind the head is a sort of hump, which is bright scarlet also.

You may find these handsome caterpillars on the leaves of hawthorn, and also on those of plum trees. When they are fully fed they spin a silken web among the leaves, and turn to chrysalids, out of which the moths hatch in July.

H

PLATE XXX

THE PALE TUSSOCK (3 and 4)

You may sometimes see this handsome moth resting on a fence in May, and "drying" its wings after coming out from the chrysalis. The female is not quite like the male, for she is generally a good deal larger, with a very much stouter body, and instead of having a dark brown stripe across the middle of her wings, as he has, she has two wavy lines, one rather before the middle, and the other rather beyond it.

The caterpillar of this moth is generally known as the "hop dog"; but I cannot tell you the reason why, for it feeds a great deal more often on the leaves of oak, lime, and hazel than it does on those of the hop. It is one of the loveliest of all our British caterpillars—very hairy, and of the most delicate pale green colour, with three bands of deep velvety black round its body. On its back are four brush-like tufts of long yellow hairs, pointing forwards, and on its tail is another still longer tuft of the same colour, which points backwards. When it is fully grown it spins a very slight silken web among the leaves, and turns to a hairy chrysalis. You may find it feeding in July and August.

PLATE XXXI

1. Lackey
3. Vapourer, male
5. Vapourer, female

2. Lackey Caterpillar
4. Vapourer Caterpillar

PLATE XXXI

THE LACKEY (1 and 2)

If you look at the twigs of apple trees during the winter time you will sometimes find that they are surrounded by bands of tiny greyish-white eggs, most neatly arranged in rows, which look just like tiny bracelets. These are the eggs of the Lackey Moth, and when they hatch a number of pretty little caterpillars make their appearance, and at once set to work to spin a big silken web among the leaves, in which they live. They are rather hairy, and have blue-grey heads with two black spots which look just like eyes, and bodies striped with white, and blue, and red, and yellow. And sometimes they are so plentiful that they strip whole branches, and even whole trees, of their leaves. When they are fully grown they spin yellow cocoons, in which a quantity of dust that looks just like powdered sulphur is mixed up, and change to smooth brown chrysalids, out of which the moths are hatched in July.

Lackey moths vary a good deal in colour, for some are light yellow, and some are dark yellow, and some are pale brown, and some are reddish-brown. Indeed, you may often catch six or eight of these moths, one after the other, and find that no two of them are quite alike.

PLATE XXXI

THE VAPOURER (3, 4, and 5)

On any warm, sunny day from the beginning of August till the middle of October you may see a little brown moth darting swiftly about, with a curious zigzag flight. First it flies for a few feet in one direction, then for a few feet in another direction, and then for a few feet in a third direction, and always at some little height from the ground. This is a male Vapourer Moth, and a very pretty little fellow he is, with bright chestnut - brown wings, and a crescent - shaped white mark in the middle of the front ones. But his mate is not in the least like him. In fact, if you were to see her, you would find it very hard to believe that she was a moth at all; for she has no wings, and looks just like a very fat grey grub. She is so fat, indeed, that she cannot even walk, and has to spend her whole life clinging to the cocoon in which she lived as a chrysalis. And when she has covered this cocoon all over with her little round white eggs she falls to the ground and dies.

The caterpillar of the Vapourer moth is very common. You may find it feeding upon the leaves of all sorts of trees and plants in the garden; and you can tell it at once by the row of little tufts of hair, just like tiny shaving-brushes, upon its back.

PLATE XXXII

1. Oak Eggar   2. Drinker

3. Drinker Caterpillar

PLATE XXXII

THE OAK EGGAR (1)

If you walk across a heath or a moor on a hot day in June you may often see a large brown moth dashing wildly about quite close to the ground. This is almost sure to be a male Oak Eggar. You can always tell him from the female by his deep chestnut-brown wings, hers being light brownish-yellow. And besides that, she is a good deal larger than he is, and has a very much stouter body.

The caterpillar of this moth is a big brown creature, which you may find feeding upon the leaves of hawthorn bushes in May. You cannot possibly mistake it for that of any other insect, for its body is covered all over with short yellow down, just like fur. If you touch it, or frighten it in any way, it at once drops to the ground and curls itself up into a ring; and then you notice a number of black bands round its body, which are really formed by the dark skin showing through the fur.

Early in June this caterpillar spins a dark brown cocoon and changes to a brown chrysalis, out of which the moth hatches about a fortnight or three weeks later.

PLATE XXXII

THE DRINKER (2 and 3)

This seems rather an odd name to give to a
moth, doesn't it? But it really belongs to the
caterpillar, which you may often see drinking
the dewdrops on the long grass on which it feeds.
It is a very hairy caterpillar, of a dark brown
colour, with yellow spots and streaks upon its
sides, and little tufts of short white down between
them. I would advise you to be very careful in
handling it, for its long hairs have a way of work-
ing themselves into one's skin, and causing big
swellings and a great deal of irritation. Indeed,
if you were to rub your eyes after handling one
of these caterpillars, you would run a good deal
of risk of losing your sight!

Drinker caterpillars are very common indeed
in some places, and you may often see them
feeding on the long grass by the roadside in
May. About the beginning of June they spin
shuttle-shaped yellow cocoons, which are always
fastened to stout grass-stems, and turn to dark
brown chrysalids, out of which the moths hatch
in July. The male moth, like that of the "oak
eggar," is a good deal smaller than the female,
and is much darker in colour.

PLATE XXXIII

1

2

1. Lappet
2. Lappet Caterpillar

PLATE XXXIII

THE LAPPET (1 and 2)

When this moth first hatches out of the chrysalis it is really a very beautiful insect, for although the wings are reddish-brown all over, they have a kind of purple bloom on them, just like that on a ripe plum. But after a day or two this bloom always gets worn off. The moth is not at all an uncommon one, and yet one hardly ever sees it. The reason is that when it sits with its wings folded together over its back, as it almost always does, it is exactly like a dead leaf. You might look straight at it from only a few inches away, and never imagine for a moment that it was really a moth. And if it is hard to see the moth, it is still harder to see the caterpillar, which flattens itself against the branches of blackthorn bushes, and looks just like a piece of rather rough bark.

You may find this caterpillar—if you look for it *very* carefully indeed—in May and June. A little before midsummer it spins a long blackish cocoon, either among the leaves of its food-plant or amongst grass quite close to the ground, and changes to a smooth black chrysalis, out of which the moth appears early in July.

PLATE XXXIV

THE SWALLOW-TAILED MOTH (1 and 2)

You may often see this handsome moth flying about in the garden on warm evenings in July; and during the daytime you may sometimes shake it out of ivy, or out of the leaves of a thick bush, in which it has taken refuge from the unwelcome daylight. It is easy to see why it is called the "Swallow-tailed" Moth, for on the hindwings are two little "tails," very much like those of the "swallow-tailed butterfly."

The caterpillar of this moth is one of those which we call "loopers," because instead of walking as other caterpillars do, they hunch themselves up into a sort of loop at every step. And sometimes they are called "stick-caterpillars," because their bodies are so like bits of twig that as long as they do not move it is very difficult indeed to see them.

If you shake the branches of a tree in summertime you will generally see several of these caterpillars swinging in the air, each at the end of a silken thread; and if you want to find that of the Swallow-tailed Moth you should look for it on willow, and lime, and elder, and pear trees. When it is fully grown it spins a cocoon just like a little hammock, and turns to a light brown chrysalis spotted with black.

PLATE XXXIV

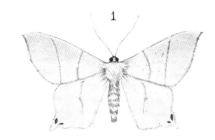

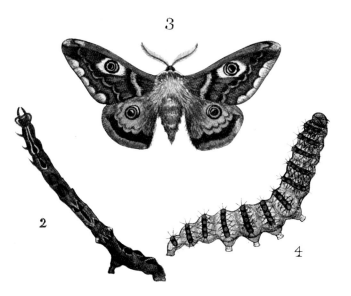

1. Swallow-tail Moth   2. Swallow-tail Caterpillar
3. Emperor   4. Emperor Caterpillar

PLATE XXXIV

THE EMPEROR (3 and 4)

This is one of the handsomest of all our British moths, and the caterpillar is even more beautiful than the moth. For it is of the brightest apple-green colour, with ten or eleven velvety black rings round its body; and every ring has a number of raised pink spots upon it, with six black bristles springing from each spot, and spreading outwards in the form of a star. You may often find it on bramble-leaves early in September, and it also feeds on blackthorn, willow, and heath.

When this lovely caterpillar has reached its full size, it spins a most curious cocoon, shaped something like a little flask, with a number of bristles inside the entrance arranged in such a way, that while the moth can crawl out quite easily when it is ready to hatch, none of its enemies can crawl in. In this cocoon the chrysalis lies all through the winter, and the moth makes its appearance in April, when you may often see it flying about in the sunshine on heaths and commons. The male is rather smaller than the female, and you can always recognise him by his brighter colouring, and his beautifully plumed feelers.

I

PLATE XXXV

THE BRIMSTONE MOTH (1)

There is a Brimstone Moth, just as there is a "brimstone butterfly," and you may find it very commonly indeed in almost any part of the country, and at almost any time from April until October, or even November. During the day-time it generally hides away among the leaves of ivy, or of some thick bush, like the "swallow-tailed moth." But you may sometimes see it resting on a fence, or on the trunk of a tree; and after dark it often comes flying into a lighted room through an open window. The caterpillar feeds on hawthorn, and blackthorn, and apple, and sometimes on bramble. It is pale brown in colour, with a bluish spot on each side of its neck, and with three little humps on its back, just like the tiny leaf-buds on a bit of twig. So although it is so common you will not find it unless you look very carefully indeed, and even the sharp eyes of the insect-eating birds often pass it by. As soon as it reaches its full size it spins a thick silken cocoon and turns into a brown chrysalis, out of which the moth appears two or three weeks later.

PLATE XXXV

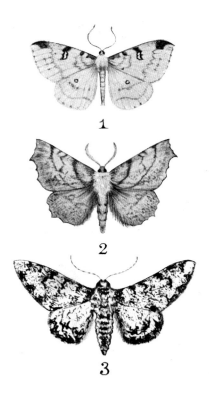

1. Brimstone
2. Canary Shouldered Thorn
3. Pepper and Salt

PLATE XXXV

THE CANARY-SHOULDERED THORN (2)

There are several different kinds of "Thorn" moths, but you can always tell the Canary-Shouldered Thorn from the others by just looking at the middle part of its body, which is thickly covered with very long hairs of a bright canary yellow. It appears on the wing in August, and is very fond of flying into a lighted room after dark. Sometimes, too, it will sit on the glass of a street-lamp and remain there all night long without moving, gazing at the flame within. If it can get inside the lamp, it will often burn its wings so badly that it cannot fly away. And just now and then you may find it sitting on a fence, or on the trunk of a tree.

The caterpillar of this moth is one of the "loopers," and is dark brown in colour, with lighter markings, and with two little humps on its back. Look for it on the leaves of birch, lime, elder, oak, and fruit trees during the month of June. About the first week in July it spins a little silken cocoon, and turns into a light brown chrysalis, with a few whitish markings.

PLATE XXXV

THE PEPPER AND SALT MOTH (3)

No doubt you will think that this is rather an odd name to give to a moth, but it is a very suitable one, for the wings of this insect really do look very much as if they had been first covered with salt, and then sprinkled thickly with black pepper. But it varies a good deal in its markings, for sometimes the wings look as if they were nearly all salt, and sometimes they look as if they were nearly all pepper. And if the moth is caught in the north of England or in Scotland, strange to say, it is nearly always much darker than when it is caught in the south.

The caterpillar, too, varies almost as much in colour as the moth. Sometimes it is reddish-brown; sometimes it is greenish-brown; sometimes it is yellowish-brown. But it always looks very much like a piece of stick; and it always has eight raised reddish spots on its back, which look just like buds before they begin to burst into leaf. You may find it in August, feeding on the leaves of lime, birch, and oak trees. In September it buries itself in the ground, and changes to a rather fat brown chrysalis, out of which the moth appears in the following May.

PLATE XXXVI

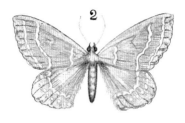

1. Willow Beauty
2. Large Emerald

PLATE XXXVI

THE WILLOW BEAUTY (1)

I am sorry to say that I cannot tell you why this moth is called the "Willow Beauty." For, in the first place, it is not a very beautiful insect. Both its front and hinder wings are greyish-brown all over, with a few wavy black lines running across them, and one pale zigzag streak near the outer margin. Certainly, one would hardly call it a "beauty." And then, in the second place, it has nothing to do with willow trees; for its grey, twig-like caterpillar feeds on the leaves of rose-bushes, and plum trees, and pear trees, and birch trees, and sometimes on those of lilac and elder, but never on the leaves of willows.

This moth is a very common one indeed in all parts of the country, and from the middle of June until the beginning of August you may see it in numbers, resting with outspread wings on fences and tree-trunks during the day, and fluttering round gas-lamps in the evening.

There is another moth which is very like the "willow beauty," but is nearly twice as big, and is rather lighter in colour. This is called the "great oak beauty," and you may sometimes see it resting on the trunks of oak trees in June.

PLATE XXXVI
THE LARGE EMERALD (2)

The "emeralds" are pale green moths with very delicate wings, and the Large Emerald is the finest and most beautiful of them all. It is almost as large as the "swallow-tail moth," and when it first comes out of the chrysalis its wings are of the most lovely green colour, with three wavy white lines across the front pair, and a scalloped white line and a row of white dots across the hinder ones. But after two or three days it begins to fade; and if you were to put it away in a collection you would most likely find after a few months that it was nearly white.

The Large Emerald is not a very common moth, but you may sometimes find it by shaking bushes and the branches of trees in June and July. The caterpillar feeds on the leaves of birch and elm, and is green in colour, with a yellow line along each side, and six pairs of little reddish bumps which look like tiny buds. About the end of May it forms a kind of cocoon by spinning together two or three leaves of its food-plant, and turns into a brownish-green chrysalis, with two rows of reddish spots on its back.

PLATE XXXVII

1. Bordered White, male   2. Bordered White, female
3. Magpie   4. Magpie Caterpillar

PLATE XXXVII

THE BORDERED WHITE (1 and 2)

If you want to find this handsome moth, the best way to do so is to shake the branches of fir trees with a long stick during the month of May. Then you are almost sure to see it flying off in a great hurry to seek for refuge somewhere else. But it never seems quite happy unless it can hide away among the needle-like leaves of a fir tree. The male is very different in appearance from the female, for his wings are either white or yellowish-white in colour, with a broad black border, while hers are orange-brown all over, with only two narrow dark bands. And, besides that, his feelers are beautifully plumed, while hers are just like threads. In fact, the male and female are so unlike one another that, if you did not know what they were, you would be almost sure to take them for two perfectly different insects.

The caterpillar of this moth is a very pretty little creature of a pale green colour, with a broad white line along the back and a bluish-white line below it; then a yellow line below that; and then a row of orange spots. You may sometimes find it in August, feeding on the leaves of fir trees.

PLATE XXXVII

THE MAGPIE MOTH (3 and 4)

This is called the Magpie Moth because its wings are chiefly black and white in colour, like the plumage of a magpie. But there are two orange bands on the front wings as well, and the body is orange, spotted with black. It varies a good deal in colouring however, for sometimes there are hardly any black markings on the wings, and sometimes there are hardly any white ones. And just now and then you may meet with a very odd Magpie Moth indeed, with the wings on one side of its body a good deal larger than those on the other!

This is a very common moth indeed, and you may shake it out of the bushes in almost any garden in July and the early part of August. And you may also find its caterpillars feeding on the leaves of currant and raspberry and gooseberry bushes. It is creamy-white in colour, with rows of large black spots, and a yellow stripe along each side, and turns into a dark brown chrysalis with orange bands round it. And it seems to have a very nasty taste, for no bird will ever attempt to eat it.

This insect is sometimes known as the Currant Moth.

PLATE XXXVIII

1. Spring Usher   2. Winter Moth, male
3. Winter Moth, female

PLATE XXXVIII

THE SPRING USHER (1)

This very pretty moth is one of the first to make its appearance after the winter is over, for you may see it resting on fences and walls in March, and sometimes even in February. But you may easily pass it by without noticing it, for it is very fond of sitting among splashes of mud, which it resembles so much that you may look straight at it from a distance of only a few feet, without seeing what it really is. It varies in colour almost as much as the magpie moth, for sometimes it is nearly white all over, and sometimes it is nearly black; but generally the wings are greyish-white, with a few narrow black stripes.

When you see one of these moths, however, you may be quite sure that it is a male; for the female has no wings at all, and looks just like a little greyish-white grub, with six rather long legs. She lays her eggs on the twigs of oak trees, and the little caterpillars hatch out in May. I cannot describe them, for they are all sorts of different colours, so that you may easily find fifteen or twenty, no two of which are quite alike.

K

PLATE XXXVIII

THE WINTER MOTH (2 and 3)

This is perhaps the very commonest of all our British moths. It simply swarms in all parts of the country, and on any mild day from the beginning of November till the end of January you may see it in hundreds, resting on fences and tree-trunks. And after dark it visits almost every street-lamp, and sits on the glass gazing at the flame within. But if you want to see the female you must look for her very carefully, for she is a little grub-like creature with hardly any wings at all, very much like that of the "spring usher," except that she is brown instead of white. You may often find her hiding in the cracks of the bark of fruit trees, to which the caterpillars sometimes do a very great deal of damage.

These caterpillars differ a good deal in colouring, for sometimes they are light green, and sometimes they are dark green, and sometimes they are smoky brown. But they always have a black stripe down the back, and three white ones on either side. There is hardly a tree or a bush on the leaves of which they do not feed, and in May and June you may often see them in thousands and thousands.

PLATE XXXIX

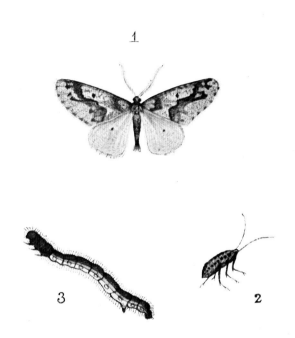

1. Mottled Umber, male   2. Mottled Umber, female
3. Mottled Umber Caterpillar

PLATE XXXIX

THE MOTTLED UMBER (1, 2, and 3)

Towards the end of October, and all through the month of November, you may often find this handsome moth resting on fences, or on the trunks of trees. But although it is so brightly coloured you may easily pass it by without seeing it, for it looks almost exactly like a piece of dead and withered leaf. The male varies a good deal in markings. Sometimes, for instance, he has no dark streaks on his wings at all, but is reddish-brown all over, sprinkled with very tiny blackish dots. But the female is always grub-like, with such very tiny wings that you can hardly see them. You can tell her from that of any other of the "winter moths" by the two rows of large black spots which run all down her yellowish-brown body.

The caterpillars of this moth are very plentiful indeed. In colour they are reddish-brown above, with a broad yellow stripe on each side, and greenish-yellow beneath. They feed upon the leaves of hazel, oak, birch, sloe, and ever so many other trees and bushes. And if you walk through a wood in May or June, after a strong wind has been blowing, you may often see numbers of them swinging in the air, each suspended from a twig or a leaf by a slender silken thread.

PLATE XL

THE GARDEN CARPET (1)

This is another of our very commonest British moths. You may find it in dozens, and even in hundreds, in almost any garden, just by shaking the bushes or the branches of the trees. And very often you may see it resting on a wall, or on a fence, or fluttering about in a lighted room at night. It is fond, too, of hiding in outhouses and sheds, or behind a piece of loose bark on the trunk of a dead tree. In fact, there is hardly any place where you may *not* find it, from the beginning of May until the end of September, and sometimes even later still. And if you wanted to catch a hundred, or five hundred, or a thousand Garden Carpets, you could very easily do so.

The caterpillars, of course, are quite as common as the moths. They are queer little stick-like creatures, and vary very much in colour, some being grey, and some light green, and some dark green, and some pale brown. But they always have several arrow-shaped dark markings upon their backs, with four or five pale blotches behind them. Look for them on nasturtium leaves, and also on those of cabbage and horse-radish plants.

PLATE XL

1

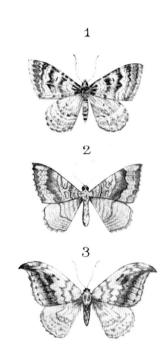

2

3

1. Garden Carpet   2. Yellow Shell
3. Pebble Hook-tip

PLATE XL

THE YELLOW SHELL (2)

I really think that this moth is even commoner than the "garden carpet." From the beginning of June till the middle of August you can hardly go into the garden without seeing it. If you look at a fence or a tree-trunk, there it is sure to be resting with outspread wings. If you shake a bush or a low plant, or the leaves of a creeper growing upon a wall, it is certain to fly out. And soon after sunset on any warm evening you may see it flying about in scores, or even in hundreds.

But although the moth is so very plentiful, one hardly ever sees the caterpillar. The reason is that it only feeds by night, and hides away all day long under stones, or beneath small clods of earth, or at the roots of grass. But if you were to go out with a lantern on a mild evening towards the end of April, and search carefully on the grass-stems, you would be able to find it without any difficulty at all. It is dull green in colour, with a darker stripe along the back, and two white ones on each side; and underneath its body it generally has a number of rose-coloured or violet spots.

PLATE XL

THE PEBBLE HOOK-TIP (3)

Five different kinds of "hook-tip" moths are found in the British Islands, and you can tell them at once by the hook-like tip to their front wings. The Pebble Hook-tip is by far the commonest of the five. If you want to find it, the best way to do so is to shake the branches of birch trees, either in May, or in August, for this is one of the "double-brooded" moths. That is, they make their appearance twice in each year, the eggs laid by the spring brood producing moths in the summer, while those laid by the summer brood produce moths in the following spring.

The caterpillar of this moth is rather curiously shaped, for its tail—which it always holds up in the air—is drawn out into quite a sharp point. It has a grey head and a light green body, with a purple stripe down the back. It feeds on the leaves of birch trees, and when it has reached its full size it doubles over a corner of one of the leaves, fastens it firmly down by means of a number of silken threads, and then turns into a chrysalis.

PLATE XLI

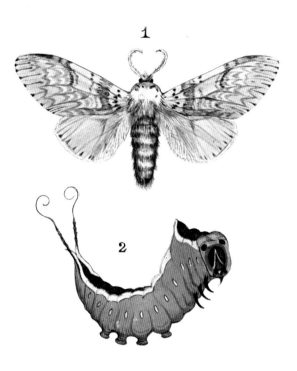

1. Puss
2. Puss Caterpillar

PLATE XLI

THE PUSS MOTH (1 and 2)

This fine and handsome moth is called the "Puss," because, when its wings are closed, it looks rather like a brindled cat. And there are two or three smaller moths which are a good deal like it; so these are known as "Kittens."

One does not very often see the Puss Moth, although it is quite a common insect. But you can easily find its caterpillars by looking for them on the leaves of poplar and willow trees in August. They are most odd-looking creatures —bright apple-green in colour, with black heads, and with white and purple stripes upon their backs and sides, and with the front part of the body drawn up into quite a large hump. In front of this hump are two big black spots, which might easily be mistaken for eyes. And at the end of the body are two long, slender horns, from each of which the caterpillar pokes out a pink, thread-like organ when it is frightened. These organs look very much like stings, but they are per-fectly harmless, so that you need not be in the least afraid to handle the insect. And the odd thing is that if two or three of these caterpillars are shut up in a box together, they nearly always nibble at one another's horns.

When the Puss Moth caterpillar is fully fed

it creeps into a chink in the bark, spins a tough silken cocoon, and changes into a chrysalis, from which the moth appears in the following May.

PLATE XLII

THE LOBSTER (1 and 2)

This seems a very odd name for a moth, doesn't it? And if you were to see the moth you would be quite sure to wonder why such a title should ever have been given to it, for it is not in the very least like a lobster. But the fact is that it has a most singular-looking caterpillar, with very long legs, five pairs of large humps on its back, and the end of its body swollen out to a huge size, with two curved horns on the top. Really it does look not unlike a lobster with a very big claw, and a great many people would be quite afraid to touch it. However, it is perfectly harmless, so that if ever you meet with it you may pick it up without the least fear of being bitten, or pinched, or stung.

This very odd caterpillar feeds on the leaves of oak, birch, and beech trees in August and September. When it has finished growing it spins two or three leaves together by means of a few silken threads, and turns into a chrysalis between them, from which the moth hatches out in the following May or June.

PLATE XLII

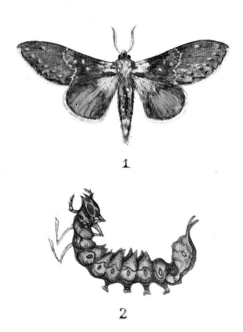

1

2

1. Lobster
2. Lobster Caterpillar

PLATE XLIII

1

2

1. Buff Tip
2. Buff Tip Caterpillar

PLATE XLIII

THE BUFF TIP (1 and 2)

Most people know the caterpillar of this moth a good deal better than they know the moth itself. I dare say that you have often seen it crawling about in August and September, always walking very fast, as though it were in a great hurry. It is a big, rather hairy creature of a dull yellow colour, with a black head, and with nine black stripes running along its body ; and you may find it in numbers, feeding on the leaves of elm, lime, and willow trees. Very often, indeed, it is so plentiful that it strips whole branches of their leaves. When it reaches its full size it comes down from the tree, wanders off to some little distance, hides away under dead leaves or at the roots of a tuft of grass, and turns into a dark brown chrysalis, out of which the moth hatches in the following May or June.

The reason why one sees this handsome moth so very much seldomer than the caterpillar is that it always rests with its wings folded closely against its body, in which position it looks just like a piece of broken stick. But you may often find it clinging to the trunk of an elm or a lime tree, or to a long grass-stem growing underneath it.

PLATE XLIV

THE FIGURE-OF-EIGHT (I)

You have only to look at this moth to see why its name was given to it, for on each of its front wings it has two large white spots with two small dark spots inside them, one above the other; so that they look very much like the figure 8. But the inner 8 is always a much neater one than the outer, which has a kind of blurred appearance, just as if a drop of water had fallen upon it and made the colours run.

This moth is quite a common one in most parts of the country, and appears on the wing in September. It only flies by night, so that one does not often see it; but it will sometimes fly into a well-lighted room on a dark, warm evening if the window is left open. You can find the caterpillar, however, without any difficulty at all. All that you have to do is to hunt for it on hawthorn or blackthorn bushes during May or the early part of June, and there you are almost sure to see it — a smoky green creature thinly covered with black hairs, and with a yellow stripe running down its back, and another along each side of its body. A little later on it spins a neat little cocoon, made partly of silk and partly of bits of bark and leaf, which it fastens underneath a twig of its food-plant. And in this it changes into a chrysalis.

PLATE XLIV

1. Figure of Eight   2. Peach Blossom
         3. Grey Dagger

PLATE XLIV

THE PEACH BLOSSOM (2)

This is really a lovely moth, for on each of its olive-brown front wings it has five large spots, which are coloured exactly like the petals of a peach. But if it is put away in a collection these spots very soon fade, unless the insect is kept in the dark, and after a few months they become almost white.

The caterpillar of this moth is a very odd-looking creature indeed, for when it is resting on a leaf of its food-plant it only makes use of its middle feet, and holds both the front ones and the hind ones up in the air! Besides this, it has quite a row of little humps on its back, the front one of which is sometimes so large that it forms a kind of hood, and partly covers the head! You may sometimes find it feeding on the leaves of bramble bushes growing in woods in August and the early part of September. When it has grown to its full size it spins a slight cocoon of silken threads among the leaves, and turns into a blackish-brown chrysalis, with a sharp little spike at the end of its body. Out of this the moth hatches in the following June or July.

PLATE XLIV

THE GREY DAGGER (3)

You cannot possibly fail to recognise this moth if you meet with it, for its front wings are of a light pearly-grey colour, with a number of black markings upon them, several of which look just like little daggers laid sideways. It is a very common insect indeed, and all through June and July you may see it resting on fences, and walls, and tree-trunks. A little later you may find the caterpillar, which is quite as easy to recognise as the moth. It has a rather hairy body, a black head with two yellow stripes upon it, and a black body, with a broad yellow streak along the back, and a number of small red streaks on each side, which are curved in the shape of a bow. Besides this, it has two humps on its back, the front one of which is black, while the hinder one is yellow; so that altogether it is a very odd-looking creature indeed. It feeds on the leaves of beech, lime, poplar, hawthorn, pear, and ever so many other trees, and is fully fed about the middle of September, when it creeps into some cranny in the bark, spins a strong silken cocoon, and turns into a chrysalis.

PLATE XLV

1. Large Yellow Underwing
2. Red Underwing

PLATE XLV

THE LARGE YELLOW UNDERWING (1)

There are several different kinds of Yellow Underwing moths, but this is by far the commonest of them all. It makes its appearance in June and July, and although it only flies by night you can easily find it during the day. All that you have to do is to go to a strawberry bed, and brush about among the leaves of the plants. Before long you are quite sure to see one of these moths running quickly about like a mouse in search of a fresh hiding-place. And, if you try to catch it, it will take to its wings, fly for a few yards, and then again settle down to seek some place of concealment among the herbage.

The caterpillars of this moth are very mischievous creatures, for they eat their way right into the hearts of cabbage and lettuce plants, and quite spoil them for the table. And as they only feed by night, and hide away beneath the surface of the ground by day, it is not at all easy to catch them. They vary a good deal in colour. Indeed, you may find them of almost any shade, from light yellowish-green to dark brown. But along the back there is always a yellow stripe, with a dark line on each side of it, while on the sides there is a row of seven or eight short black streaks.

You may find these caterpillars from March till the beginning of June.

PLATE XLV

THE RED UNDERWING (2)

As you will see by the illustration, this is a very fine and handsome moth indeed; but when it is at rest it is very difficult indeed to see it, for the bright red hind-wings are quite covered up by the grey front ones, so that it looks exactly like the bark of the trees on which it is so fond of sitting. If you want to catch it, the best place to look for it is on the trunks of willow trees, in August and September. But sometimes you may find it on fences, and just now and then it will fly through an open window into a well-lighted room by night.

The caterpillar of this beautiful moth feeds on the leaves of willows, sallows, and poplars. It is rather oddly shaped, for its back is very much arched, while its lower surface is almost flat. And, if you touch it, it only clings more tightly to its foothold, instead of curling up into a ring and dropping to the ground, as most caterpillars do. In colour it is ashy-grey, and generally has two dark, wavy stripes running along the back. When it is fully fed it spins a silken cocoon, either between two leaves or in a crack in the bark, and changes to a reddish-brown chrysalis covered with purple bloom, just like that on a ripe plum.

PLATE XLVI

1

2

1. Pine Beauty
2. Old Lady

PLATE XLVI

THE PINE BEAUTY (1)

This is a really lovely moth, which always comes out in the early spring. If you want to find it, you should hunt for it on the trunks of pine trees, about three or four feet from the ground. But you will have to look for it very carefully indeed, for it is one of the most difficult of all moths to see. The reason is that when its wings are folded it looks exactly like a little bit of the tree trunk from which the outer bark has been knocked off; so that you might easily look straight at it from only two or three feet away and yet never notice it. But after dark it is very fond of feasting upon the sweet juices of sallow catkins, or "palms," as so many people call them. And if you were to shake one of these bushes over an open umbrella on a warm evening about the beginning of April, you would very likely find a Pine Beauty lying inside it with its wings folded, and pretending to be dead.

The caterpillar of this moth is either pale brown, or bright green, or dark green in colour, with five white stripes running along its body, one on the back, and two on each side. It feeds on the leaves of the Scotch fir in June and July.

PLATE XLVI

THE OLD LADY (2)

If you were to ask me why this moth should be called the "Old Lady," I am not quite sure that I could tell you. But I think the reason must be that old ladies mostly dress in dark grey, or dark brown, or black, which are just the colours of the wings of the moth. It is quite a common insect in most parts of the country, and yet one very seldom sees it; for it always hides away during the day-time in some dark nook or cranny, where it is not very easily found. Perhaps the best place to look for it is inside a boat-house, or a summer-house, or a shed, about the end of July or during the first or second week in August. And if you find it, and frighten it away, it will very often come back again in a short time to exactly the same spot.

The caterpillar of this moth feeds on the leaves of various fruit-trees, on which you may find it in May. It has a smooth, velvety body of a dingy brown colour, with a number of paler and darker markings, and on the back is a row of eight dark spots shaped just like lozenges.

PLATE XLVII

1. Pink-barred Sallow   2. Angle-shades

3. Silver Y.

PLATE XLVII

THE PINK-BARRED SALLOW (1)

This is one of the most beautiful of all our British moths, for its front wings are of the most lovely orange-yellow, with a broad purple-pink band running across them, and several blotches and spots of the same colour on each side of it, while the hind-wings are light yellow, with a darker border. It comes out in September and October, and the best way to find it is to search on ivy blossoms on a warm, still evening, by the help of a bull's-eye lantern. A great many moths are very fond of these blossoms, and sometimes you may see them feasting on the nectar in hundreds, or even in thousands, with their little eyes gleaming like balls of coloured fire in the light of the lantern. And just here and there among them you are almost sure to notice a Pink-barred Sallow.

The caterpillar of this moth feeds first of all upon the catkins of sallow bushes. But when they begin to die off it goes down to the ground, and feeds upon the leaves of plantains and other low plants instead. In colour it is reddish-brown, with a number of brown, red, yellow, and white dots all over its body.

M

PLATE XLVII

THE ANGLE-SHADES (2)

This is a very common moth indeed, but a very difficult one to see. For when it is at rest it always folds its yellowish-brown and olive-green wings closely round its body, and looks so like a shrivelled piece of dead leaf that it is very hard indeed to believe that it is really a moth. It is double-brooded, coming out first in May, and then again in September and October. But it always seems much more plentiful in the autumn than in the spring, and you can generally find it in numbers by looking on the blossoms of ivy on a warm evening. And you will notice that the hairs on the "thorax," or middle part of its body, are so long that they form a kind of ruff all round its neck.

The caterpillar of the Angle-shades is either grass-green in colour or light brown, powdered thickly with tiny white dots, and with a pale white line running down the middle of its back. It feeds on nettle, chickweed, primrose, mullein, and other low plants, and when it is fully grown makes a light cocoon just beneath the surface of the ground, in which it turns to a shiny reddish-brown chrysalis.

PLATE XLVII

THE SILVER Y (3)

This is a very common moth indeed, and if you walk through a field of clover or lucerne in August or the early part of September, you may sometimes kick it out of the herbage at nearly every step that you take, until Silver Y moths are buzzing about you almost like bees. You can easily recognise it, for in the middle of each of its front wings it has a mark shaped something like the letter Y, and looking just as if it were made of polished silver. And you may also see the moth flying over flowers in the evening, while after dark it often comes into a lighted room. Indeed, one really wonders whether Silver Y moths ever go to sleep at all!

The caterpillar of this moth is shaped very much like that of the burnished brass, and walks in just the same curious way. It is rather hairy, and is bright apple-green in colour, with six narrow white lines running along its back, and a yellow stripe on either side. It feeds on all kinds of garden herbs and low plants, and when it is fully fed it spins a white cocoon among the leaves, and turns into a shiny black chrysalis, from which the moth generally hatches out about three weeks later.

PLATE XLVIII

THE BEAUTIFUL YELLOW
UNDERWING (1)

This is really a most lovely little moth. It is something like a very, very small "large yellow underwing." But instead of having the front wings plain light or dark brown, with hardly any markings at all, it has them bright red-brown with pure white spots and wavy lines, while the hind-wings are of the brightest possible yellow, with a broad edging of glossy black.

If you want to see this very pretty insect, you can easily do so. All that you have to do is to ramble over a heathy common on a hot, sunny day in May or June, and you are sure, before long, to notice a Beautiful Yellow Underwing flying about over the heather. It hardly looks like a moth. It looks more like a brightly-coloured little bee. And it flies so quickly that you will have some little difficulty in catching it.

The caterpillar of this moth feeds on heather and bilberry, and is bright green in colour, with five white lines running along its body. Down its back is a line made up of short white streaks. Below this, on each side, is another line, made up of white spots. And lower down still is a third line, also made up of spots, which run up and down in a zigzag. Look for this caterpillar in August.

PLATE XLVIII

1. Beautiful Yellow Underwing   2. Orange Underwing
3. Burnished Brass

PLATE XLVIII

THE ORANGE UNDERWING (2)

There are really two kinds of Orange Under-
wings, the light and the dark. But they come
out at the same time, and fly about together,
and are so much alike that it is not at all easy
to tell the one from the other. The time to look
for them is about the middle or end of March,
and then, if you go into a large wood on a
warm, sunny morning, you may sometimes see
them flying about among birch trees. They are
very fond, too, of visiting sallow, or "palm,"
bushes, and sucking the sweet juices from their
golden-yellow catkins. But the moment that
the sun is clouded over they seem to disappear,
and you will see them no more until it begins
to shine again.

The caterpillars of both the Orange Under-
wings are dull green in colour, with yellow lines
on their backs and sides, and when they walk
they hunch their bodies up into loops, just like
the "stick" caterpillars of such moths as the
"swallow-tail" and the "willow beauty." That
of the Light Orange Underwing feeds on aspen,
and that of the Dark Orange Underwing upon
birch. You may find both in June and July.

PLATE XLVIII

THE BURNISHED BRASS (3)

This moth well deserves its name, for across its greyish-brown or reddish-brown front wings its has two broad bands of golden-green, which shine just like a piece of highly polished brass. It is "double-brooded," coming out first in June and then again in August, and flies soon after sunset on warm, still evenings. If you want to catch it, the best place to look for it is over beds of nettles, where you may often see it flying backwards and forwards until it is too dark to see at all. But sometimes it will fly through an open window into a lighted room, and buzz about in the most excited way round the lamp or the gas-flame.

The caterpillar of this pretty moth feeds upon stinging-nettle, dumb-nettle, and burdock, and sometimes also upon thistle and wild mint. When it is not walking it always rests with its front legs held up in the air, and its body gets stouter and stouter from the head almost to the tip of the tail. It is apple-green in colour, with a number of white marks on its back shaped just like the letter V.

Printed by BALLANTYNE, HANSON & Co.
Edinburgh & London